Thank you to Bill and Team Larder for the free cake, Cedarwood Coffee for the delicious coffee, Damson Poets for the inspiration and monthly events, Tim Linton and Harriet Skully for the illustrations, Scarlet Rains (@didanartist) for assistance with the technical stuff, Sean Green and Jonny Cosmo for bringing this book together and thank you to the writers who have contributed, this wouldn't exist without you all.

Welcome by "Just Write"

"Just Write" is a humble, Preston-based writing workshop. The group consists of a wide variety of unique and wonderful characters. All with their our own stories, experiences, and ways of expression. Meeting every Saturday, they *just write* together. Sharing hot drinks and hot topics, which are then turned into a prompt to write about. The group is not just a bunch of wannabe writers in a room at the back of a cafe. We have become a community; and a support network for people who may have found themselves lost and downtrodden. This anthology sets to focus in on this with a theme of mental health. With this collection we seek to inspire hope, perseverance and possibly some wisdom to our fellow mental health fighters. Each writer in this anthology has their own tales to tell and each is just as important as the next.

This anthology will consist of poetry, prose and song lyrics; which hope to send positivity or inspire artistic expression to the readers who may need it.

So, without further ado, let's begin.

With love,

the 'Just Write' writers.

Contents

Sam Arthur

Samuel Arthur (Street Name: Sam, Gamer Name: Genepool) lives in Lancaster with his family and cat.

Sam used to write fiction up until a few years ago when he suffered a bad turn of Depression and lost all his self-confidence in his own writing abilities. He has since tried without much luck to get back into writing fiction, where he would like to get to, and most of all enjoy once again.

In his spare time, he does enjoy writing on his blog (https://thingsilike.live), where he posts film reviews and other things too. He really enjoys writing large analytical blog posts on his favourite Monster Movies. Sam's work has been featured in several collections, including Red Rose Eclipse, Seasonal Shorts, and Love Literally. He has also self-published his own books (Tyrannosaur, and The Ducks!) onto Amazon.

His other achievements include being a Two-Time Semi-Finalist at the Preston Short Story Slam, coming second in the Alumni category in the Red Rose Eclipse Competition, and winning the Tea Tray Dueling World Championship! He is also quite possibly the only person in Lancashire, if not the entire Country to have watched all 36 current Godzilla films!

Blanket of Comfort

A blanket of comfort,
For those who are lost.
A mug of kindness
For those who need help.
A hug of strength,
For those who need picking up.
A smile of joy,
For those who have forgotten theirs.
A heart of love,
For those who need hope.
This is a friend!

A Little Bubble

Bubble,
A little bubble,
Floating through the air,
A mixture of soap and water,
Getting higher and higher.
Bubble,
A little bubble,
Dipped in solution,
Blown through a wand,
Gathering formation.
Bubble,
A little bubble,
Blown by a boy,
A young boy,
With a smile on his face.
Bubble,
A little bubble,
Blown by a boy,
Much older now,
Older than a little bubble.
Bubble,
A little bubble,
Alone in the sky,
Much like the little boy,
Now more than 20-years old.
Boy,
An older boy,
Alone in the world,
No end in sight,
Unlike a bubble popping.
Boy,
An older boy,
Blows more than one bubble,
The bubble is no longer alone,
And soon, neither will the boy.

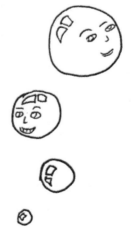

3

Cloak of Sadness

A dark cloak of sadness,
Telling lies as if it was reality.
A dark pit of worthlessness,
Bringing down the strongest warrior.
A shadow of broken lives,
Killing all hope.
A mace of heartbreak,
A shield of defiance
Impenetrable and unstoppable.
That is depression!

What are you doing?

What are you doing?
This isn't why you turned on the laptop?
Is this what it's going to be now?
Looking through Wikipedia?
Searching for videos on YouTube?
Checking to see if there's any new notifications on Facebook?
Checking emails for competition results?
What are you doing?
Why aren't you working?
Why aren't you spending your time more productively?
What are you scared of?
What is there to worry about?
Your Future?
Your worried about work?
The Job you do?
Rather than the Career you want?
I know you are sad!
I know you are in Pain!
February was a rough month!
Always is!
But now it's March!
February 2018 is dead!
It's not coming back!
I know work is a struggle for you!
You think everyone is out to get you!
That they're setting you up to fail!
You don't exactly enjoy it!
But there are at least some people you like there!
And they like you!
Even if you don't know it!
I know you spend so much time by yourself!
I know you feel isolated and alone!
I know you struggle without others around you!

I know you have had a rough experience with relationships!
But you do have friends!
It may not be a lot!
But some Friends is better than none!
Yes, some of them are far away!
But others are close by!
And they care so much about you!
I know you have been ill for a good long time now!
Since 2016!
Or even 2015!
It's a long time to be sad!
To be down!
To be Depressed!

And sometimes it feels like it will never heal!
Never Go Away!
Never leave you alone!
But look how far you have come!
Things are better!
You are better!
Life is filled with ups and downs!
And life can go wrong!
And bad things do happen!

But that doesn't stop good things from happening!
Bad things don't have to ruin your life!
Bad things can make you stronger!
If you let them!
You used to be so strong!
You used to carry so much weight!
So much worry!
You kept it inside!
So you could be a strong one for others!
To care for others!
Look after those you cared about!
It was only natural that it would all erupt!
You couldn't have kept it all in for eternity!

It was breaking you apart!
And you reached Breaking point!
Everyday feels like a struggle!
A struggle to keep going!
You can't see a future for yourself!
You see no direction!
No Path!
And you're afraid that by going forward, the horrors of the past
will return!
Like you will end up back there!
No future!
No Hope!
How do you know?
It might go that way!
It might not!
How will you know if you don't try?
If you don't experience!
It might turn out bad!
But it might turn out great!
It could be Fantastic!
Even better maybe!
Why not try it out?
What's stopping you?
Fear?
Fear of the unknown?
Or fear of the known!
Yes the past had some bad points!
But there was also some good!

You experienced the bad!
And you're afraid you might go back there!
But what happens if you don't?
Would you be disappointed?
Disappointed that your prediction wasn't true?
You care so much for so many people!
So do they!
You may not see it sometimes!

But it's true!
And they just want the best for you!
You feel as though you are meant to fail!
That the world needs someone like you!
Someone to abuse!
Someone to bully!
Someone to hurt!
You think that's how its been set up!
That is your meaning!

That is your point!
Your purpose in life!
Would your friends think that?
Do you think they want that for you?
A coin has two sides!
So does life!
Up!
and Down!
But why should you always be down?
Or feel like it's all down?
Surely there is an up?
You are a good person!
And an amazing friend!
You care so much for your friends!
And if you treated yourself, as much as you do to them!
Imagine how amazing everything could be?
You worried about the negatives of trying!
As if something bad will always happen!
And you will always fail no matter how hard you try!
Is that really true?
Why not give something a go!
If you don't try, you will never know!
If you don't enjoy it, do something else!
There are things you like doing!
Others you used to, but haven't done in a while!
And with a bit of work, you are able to pull off some amazing
things!

You have done it once!
Why couldn't it happen again?
You have been ill!
Ill for a long time!
And some illnesses don't cure overnight!
Some take time!
So give yourself some time!
Allow yourself time!
If you feel better!
Great!
If you need more time!
Fine!
Take as much time as you need!
No body wants to see you ill!
Nobody wants you to hurt yourself!
Or kill yourself!
They just want the best for you!
And when you think you're ready!
When you feel yourself once more!
You will be you!
You will be Amazing!
Life may be in a regular cycle!
Its easy to do the same thing over and over again!
And it is hard to break free!
But wouldn't it be nice to be free?
Imagine what you could do?
You have come along way!
And your feeling strange!
You have opened up!
Let out so much!
Let go of so much hardship and stress!

Maybe now is a time to do something different!
To enjoy yourself!
Remember, life has it's downs!
But it also has its ups!
And if you spend so much time down!

Imagine how many ups there could be!
Perhaps more than Down!
You just have to let yourself experience them!
Embrace them!
You could be strong again!
Stronger than ever!
But don't worry about letting your issues out!
You have friends!
People who care so much about you!
And are always there for you!
Just find them!
Talk to them!
Friends are always there for each other!
And while you have been ill!
That doesn't need to become your life!
If a cold can be cured!
Then Sadness!
Loneliness!
Depression!
Why not them also!
Try and break the cycle!
Try and do something different!
Be free!
If you aren't feeling strong enough!
Try again!
Just keep trying!
WREAK HAVOC!
Let the world know you are here!
And you are just as important as everyone else!
Show the world who you are!
Who you can be!
And who you will become!
Be Great!
Be Amazing!
But above all, be Happy!
There is a lot of sadness in the world!
But there is also a lot of Happiness!

Be Brave!
Be Strong!
Be Adventurous!
And above all!
Be You!

Sarah F. W. Hunter

In Sarah Hunter's writings, nature becomes both a muse and a teacher, offering lessons of resilience, harmony, and the interconnectedness of all living things. Inspired by the landscapes of the Lancashire Fells, northern woodlands and the coast of North Wales, Sarah seeks to inspire exploration, curiosity, and joy in the great outdoors.

Sarah also writes social media post and blogs for RSPB Ribble Estuary, runs writing for well-being events through her company Creative-Wellbeing and is a huge fan of all poetry from Spike Milligan to Rabindranath Tragore.

The Second Wound

The tide breaks on the shore,
Breaks over rocks,
Over and over,
Perpetual.
Time and tide surging forward to the pulse
Of the cosmic metronome.
Achieving the barely perceptible rearrangement of the Earth.
Erode,
Carry,
Deposit.
What is the scope of your intention?
The evolution of this game?
Is satisfaction within your grasp, but never held?
Purpose,
Resolution,
Punishment?
Did you feel the deep wound of those which were spoken
to aid you?
Did they strike at your flinching heart?
Create,
Criticise,
Remake.
Did you feel the thread of Clotho as you traced your way
here to break me?
And that in the breaking, my ancient self was healed.
The cracks and fractures, gleaming and glorious.
The kintsugi of my soul.
Broken,
Re-joined,
Gilded.

Tim Linton

Tim was a civil engineering technician who later went to work in waste disposal and highway maintenance. Due to becoming ill with M.E. (otherwise known as chronic fatigue syndrome), he could no longer get back to work. This led to a long battle with depression.

Poetry, visual art and music became an important part of his life, providing a newfound ability to express himself. Tim generally writes quirky and humorous poems to bring laughter and smiles to those around him; he also writes poetry about peace, nature and people. Tim has also has two-hundred poems published in magazines.

Tim has struggled in the past to write about himself, but with the help of the Just Write workshop, he has found the courage to write more personal poetry and about his struggles. Tim is also the creator of a poetry group in his hometown, which brings fellow writers together to express themselves. Within his poetry group and the Just Write workshop, he has made new friends and came to realise that he is not alone in his struggles.

Odd Ball

Don't play God
With someone who
seems odd.
Make it your mission
to be quiet and listen.
They are mentally ill and have
an emotional hill to climb. So please
Be kind. They have an illness of
the mind.

Outcast

If you're not part
of the pack.
If you're not
one of the gang.
If you don't fit in.
I'm ok with that.
I know how that
feels. It's an unfair
deal. So, let me
just say, in so
many ways, I
think you're great,
and you must
never, ever hate
yourself.

Fight

When you feel you can't cope.
When you feel there is no hope.
When you can't see the light at the end of the tunnel.
Fight, fight, fight, with all your might.
Look for happiness in the smallest things.
Look for brightness in everything.
I hope that someday you will be swimming in
a river of happiness.

Crying

Don't ever feel ashamed to cry.
I am proud of you for crying.
Crying is like rain dripping on leaves.
Crying is like a waterfall splashing on rocks.
Crying is like sea swishing on sand.
Crying is natural.
Crying is healing.

My fabulous fantasy

Let it be me
in a fantasy world,
with a wave of
the hand, transport
me to Wonderland.
Where reality is
shattered and
nothing really matters.

Let it be the
Mad Hatter,
with all his crazy
patter, and make
no mistake, when
I start to shiver
and shake,
that's when I'll
splatter you with
biscuits, tea
and cake.

Daz Pearce

Daz Pearce is a performance poet and musician who hails from Preston, UK. Amongst his poetry works are the collections named Provoked, Encyclopedia Platonica and Fangless – as well as a fourth collection under the working title of Supernova which should be released in the Autumn 2023.

Daz cites alternative music, angst, individualism, and human stupidity as his biggest influences – he has also been writing and recording music since he was seventeen, performing and releasing material under his own name as well as his most recent musical moniker, the Besotted. His most well-known songs include 'Poptarts' and 'I'm in love with a neurotypical'. Both which can be found on his socials.

Daz describes himself as someone who would rather be happily single than unhappily married. He is a Pescetarian and supports Preston North End FC.

Fatal Discard

Fatal discard, fatal discard
didn't try hard enough, tried too hard
Fatal discard, fatal discard
said you were ugly, called you a retard
Fatal discard, fatal discard
inevitable breakup, been on the cards
Fatal discard, fatal discard
I just hope that you're not too scarred

His love was some kind of anonym
yeah an unrepentant sinner
The love of his life eluded him
'til he looked in the mirror
His love's a cryptocurrency
he keeps it is his coffer
Yeah he's happy with you currently
'til he gets a better offer

Fatal discard, fatal discard
didn't try hard enough, tried too hard
Fatal discard, fatal discard
said you were ugly, called you a retard
Fatal discard, fatal discard
treated you with blatant disregard
Fatal discard, fatal discard
what once were dreams now lie in shards

So this is a sadly familiar lyric
yeah a tale of ache and pain
When you've invested in the vampiric
you might just end up drained

By the time you've got your sanity back

and realised that he's no good
One too many nights down the fangshack
now you're running out of blood

Fatal discard, fatal discard
didn't try hard enough, tried too hard
Fatal discard, fatal discard
said you were ugly, called you a retard
Fatal discard, fatal discard
inevitable breakup, been on the cards
Fatal discard, fatal discard
I just hope that you're not too scarred

Now let this be your last opponent
grab this chance and seize this moment
You're better than what he was inflicting
You're so much better than being a victim
Now let this be your last opponent
grab this chance and seize this moment

You're better than what he was inflicting
You're so much better than being a victim

The Co-dependence Rap

Crash course in catastrophe
a car crash of the soul
Life lesson in emotional regression
right down that rabbit hole
Just change all your clothes on demand
deduction is divisible
Ditch self-esteem to chase some dream
of a black cat that's invisible
You've horsepower I can dream of
this Lada's been well lapped
Guess who's got the right to play God
in the codependent rap?
So smile and play the nice guy
then go eat that cold fish
Subservience rules amongst us fools
this is our favourite dish
You touch tyrannosaur's torso
punching out of your depth
When shit flies nobody hears your cries
a brave face must be kept
Now choking, nerves like cheese wire
anxiety's on tap
You could just get killed by the crossfire
in the codependent rap
I know my place within this race
will always be worth less
Have read the code of our fixed abode
the answer's always yes
Right now there is no such thing
as healthy self-respect
With stress ball squeezed I'll people please
and scrape like some subject
Love how you talk so tough and terse

23

can't get enough of this crap
Pretty please let me reel off one last verse
of the codependent rap?
To breathe out's much verboten
without express permission
A ruthless trade, some deal's been made
now sold out to submission

Been noticed I'm not quite myself
am not nearly looking neat
Sentimentality saps your vitality
when it's a strictly one way street
Can't remember feeling less beautiful
one day I could just snap
Might book myself an early funeral
at the codependent rap
Raconteur feels real resentment
for the day that you went zap
My death might bring contentment
post the codependent rap
For far from the first fucking time
life's given me a slap
Psychological flaw, the usual crime
called the codependent rap
Though I know the rules of this game
all I did was stress and flap
Just like a moth to a fucking flame
through a codependent rap
A nervous breakdown's ringing
her flag on my mind map
It's a broken man she'll be bringing
to the codependent rap
Y'know if I didn't have insomnia
I'd nail a needed nap
Exhaustion's stuck one on yer
in the codependent rap
I've convinced myself that I need you

hey I'm a complicated chap
Poor pathetic creature feeds you
eat this...codependent rap
My perpetual pad in purgatory
now feels like a deathtrap
One March this mess might murder me

that's the codependent rap
Past time I went got some therapy
a misanthropic mishap
Take a running jump from jeopardy
end the codependent
codependent
codependent
codependent
rap

Vicarious

Vicarious, big bad bore of the barstool
fanning the flames towards every fool
Whether the subject's subtraction or subsidence
he's right in the action with expert guidance
Unquestioned credentials, needs no introduction
so sit in silence, await his instruction
"If I were you", well for the next hour he is
a mentoring masterclass, not to be missed
Viciously vicarious, noisily nefarious
but unlike him, your state is precarious
So you get to it post predictable pre-amble
it's the end of Bullseye and he's shouting GAMBLE
Is it fear of rejection, you frightened of failure?
Suggests you grow yourself some new genitalia
What's the worst that can happen, the worst she can say?
Well nothing, not for Vicarious anyway
Screams repeatedly "WITHOUT LOVE YOU ARE
NOTHING"
and minus Vicarious you are not worth loving
Viciously vicarious, noisily nefarious
bullying, harassment – it's just not fair, this
Hmmm...I hear how it makes you horribly hateful
and the last thing I want is to sound ungrateful
But remind me why I should follow your course
aren't you on your third (or is it fourth) divorce?
Sadly, I've forgotten these great works you did
was it humanitarian, helping Haitian kids?
Olympic medal maybe, Nobel Peace Prize?
None of the above – oh, there's a fucking surprise
Viciously vicarious, noisily nefarious
if you weren't bothering me I'd find this hilarious
So before you catcall the rest of the class
take a look at that house of yours, made of glass

Administering advice from your throne
answer to everybody's problems – except your own
"If I were you" - well you're not, can't you see?
So don't you dare live vicariously through me

You're the last rat I'd reach to if I had it rough
so for once in your life, please, shut the fuck up
Viciously vicarious, noisily nefarious
just fuck off for reasons numerous and various

drops mic

Emasculation (Radio Edit)

What does it mean to be male
in the twenty first century?
What does it mean to be male?
Who am I meant to be?
I don't seek to be shifty
and some stats you cannot hide
If you're male and under fifty
your most likely killer is...suicide
Sometimes guys just feel worthless
like they have missed their calling
Lacking a sense of purpose
to be so bereft is beyond appalling
So...confronting complication
mit kein hesitation
et sans procrastination
let's re-evaluate emasculation
You'll find this liberating
and yeah rather revealing
The news you've been awaiting
it's finally ok for boys to have feelings
The truth hits close to your home
might be a tad intrusive
but emotions and Y chromosomes
ought not be considered mutually exclusive
So...confronting complication
mit kein hesitation
et sans procrastination
let's re-evaluate emasculation
So he called me a wimp and not a proper man
said he's no interest in why
Beneath him to try to understand
all he knows is that 'proper men' never cry
She told me to man up, get over it

and to pull myself together
Insensitive? Yes babe, just a bit.
So please exit my existence. Forever

What does it mean to be male
in the twenty first century?
What does it mean to be male?
Who am I meant to be?

You might find yourself fuming
comes to all of us sometimes
Just demonstrates you're human
mate, it's fine occasionally to not be fine
A fly lands in your ointment
it seems some hope has gone
So... are you a disappointment?
Hey... having a failure does not make you one
So... confronting complication
mit kein hesitation
et sans procrastination
let's re-evaluate emasculation
So...confronting complication
mit kein castration
et sans humiliation
let's re-evaluate emasculation
let's re-evaluate emasculation

Sean Green

Sean is a Mancunian born, Blackpoolian raised spoken-word poet, who writes under the pseudonym 'heavenhead'.

School grades played second fiddle to performing arts and punk-rock bands. Mental illness became a frequent burden in his life, which led to a diagnosis of a mental health disorder at aged twenty-seven.

With the help of local authorities and support networks, Sean achieved a degree in Counselling and Psychotherapies and then went on to work in mental health recovery for the NHS and Samaritans; helping others the way he was helped. He is currently pursuing a new career away from mental health and learning other artistic mediums, including photography and filmmaking.

You can find Sean on Instagram on his art page, @heavenheadhere.

Bipoletry

Call me the manic man
All mighty and moody
I move boulders with my mind
I can control you're feeling

I could steal your girlfriend
Outperform you at sex
I am you... but a bit better
I can beat you at Chess

A midnight marauder
I'll sleep when I'm dead
I dance with the vultures
They feed *me* instead

The paper is smoking
My poetry is the best
My words are on fire
Like my whisky breath

A Freudian fetish
My superego is slacking
I split the mind's atom
Yet my body is cracking

A world on the shoulders
Hunchbacked and bruised
Kneeling in panic
Handcuffed by blues.

Some call me a boobytrap

Some call me a boobytrap
A million microfibers
Wrapped meticulously
Over and over
Into an elegant shape
A strand of DNA
with a fistful of knots
Wear me as a necklace
a few sizes too small
So, so tight
Blood-rushed blush
A horseshoe spine
Step on this stool with me
Let's play see-saw
like we did as kids
Some call me a boobytrap
A means to an end
A sweet relief from ourselves
Let's slowly fade to black
End credits. The final frame
A sudden fall from earth
Just to float back up again

A4

There is paper stuck to my wall
Some with tape
Some with sheer luck
They hang at an angle
& for dear life
Ripped at the edges
I ready their fall
Yet, the days roll on by
& I awake to empty carpet

I wish I was as resilient
as tape.
I am more like the A4
Fragile, easily torn apart
People see right through me
I let the darkness seep in
My memories, fictitious
I am riddled with bad poetry
Nicotine and coffee
stain my pretty features
A book, better left unread
No, a pamphlet
My life story fits on a page
I will not meet your expectations
Feel free to judge me by my cover.

The Do's and Don'ts of Doing

We have been observing you
and have grown quite concerned
You're looking tired, looking lazy
looking significantly worse
So, we have come together to provide
you with a little list
A list of things you *should* and *shouldn't* do
to feel better.

Number one
Don't daydream Sean
Put down that piece of paper
That pencil isn't helping you
and neither's the eraser
You cannot rub out all your problems
Like you did with all your friends.

Next comes *number two*
Wake up at a reasonable hour
Then maybe... take a shower
...No, four in the afternoon does not constitute as *reasonable.*
Oh, don't sit at the bottom and cry
You're wasting precious time
and precious water
Think of the endangered sea otters!
Think Sean, do you ever stop to *think* Sean
Or are you really that one dimensional.

All you do is sit in bed
Submersed in self-serving poem verses
You cannot change the past
and hope that everything reverses
Oh, which reminds me...
...*number three*
Learn to be green, think of the trees

Why don't *you* think of the trees?
They're our oxygen Sean
We *all* need them to breathe
So stop wasting precious tissue on
your selfish needs.

Number four
Don't you want a girlfriend?
Or a partner, or a wife?
Fuck, we'll settle for a boyfriend
if you just go get a life
You've been single four years and
you're over 25
What do we have to do to get your
priorities right?

Finally, *number five*
Just stop feeling depressed
No one is impressed that your life is a mess
You can *WALK* can't you?
You can *TALK* can't you?
You can add 2+2, use a loo
and wipe your own arse can't you?
You have opposable thumbs yet
you use them for dumb poems
When you have *all* the tools to succeed
So why don't you follow my lead
and be happy like me?
Then maybe you'll be
as successful as me.

But remember
we tell you this
...because we care.

(I'm)possible

It is like it was meant to be
Everything lines up perfectly
From conception
To history
To inevitability
We are what we are
By circumstance
luck, chance
It was meant to be
If your life feels disconnected
Remember, winning... began at birth
Remember, love is sacred
It is formed in many shapes
A dog
A mother
A chocolate cake
A woman, you just met
who you walked home from McDonald's
to keep the creeps at bay
Who you shared a gaze with
for three seconds longer than the norm
When you realise
you have just beaten the odds
seven billion to one
It's like it was meant to be
So here I am, writing a poem
about this epiphany
which sprung to mind from a thought
That when two people kiss
their heads make the shape of a heart.

It is meant to be.

Charlie Smith

Charlie Smith is a poet and aspiring author from Preston and is excited to begin sharing more of her work with the world.

Charlie is heavily influenced by her experiences of neurodiversity, mental health difficulties, and being a part of the LGBTQIA+ community. She likes creating pieces that cover hard topics, but most of them are also filled with hope. She has been performing original spoken word poems at open mics and various events, beginning of her poetry and writing journey and we can't wait to see where it leads!

Reasons Not to Die

Don't do it.
They say.
No matter how it hurts.
Think of all the reasons not to die.
Like your family, your friends, and the ones you hold dear.
Think about how sad they will be,
How you will pass on that hurt.
But what about me?
I don't want to hurt them but your words make me feel guilty.
I don't want this hurt to cling to me.
Do you know what it's like to wake up every day and feel every
bone
Aching to leave?
Every muscle tired of trying, every neuron hiding away.
I let the light in only to feel numb to its rays.
But, alas I kept trying and trying turned to surviving
And surviving turned to fighting until eventually...
I stopped looking for reasons not to die
And started looking for reasons to stay alive.
Not just for others, but for me.
For the sunlight that hits my face on crisp winter walks.
For the times I laugh until my cheeks hurt with my best friend,
Folding into each other in hysterics like yin and yang.
The tears of grief and the sting of pain
All reminders I am here and I feel and I am lucky just to be.
I am happy to just be.
On imperfect days when nothing seems to go right,
What a joy it is that there was even a chance it could.
There will be days you want to give up.
Where you fight for your life.
But keep on fighting until the good days outweigh the bad and you
find
Solace in your sad, because it just shows you cared.

Reasons to stay alive:
Number one.
I get to be *me*.

The monsters in my closet

There is a doorway in my house.
I stare at it every night and pray its wooden frame remains closed.
It's hard as a child when the monsters behind your closet door
Stare at you each night.
But it's even harder as an adult realising the real monsters
Lie in plain sight and call you by your name
And have a kind smile
And feel like a friend.
There is a doorway in my house.
I guard it with my life, I rearrange my room so
All the furniture sits in the way of me and it.
Of me and you, I padlocked and barricaded
And picked splinters out of my wounded arms
From where I tried to keep it closed.
There is a doorway in my house.
It opens every night. Sometimes every day.
And each time I pretend that it doesn't
I pretend it's all ok, that the monsters
Are at bay, that the lights are all on and it's not
Just me and my demons fighting in the dark.
Except my demon wears your skin and has your eyes
And I've convinced myself it isn't really you.
Except it was. Except it is.
And the pain and the malice all came from the palms
Of a friend.
There is a doorway in my house,
And if I am honest, the more I think about it the more its
Plywood gates open and make way for the memories
Of how you hurt me in the dark.
Like a predator. Like a coward.
There is a doorway in my house.
I think it's finally time I face the truth,
I wail and I scream.

I have clung onto this place I called home
For so long, I think it's finally time to let go.
I am only clinging to the memory of the girl I was before you
And she is gone. But I can make way,
For a new woman and a new me.
There is a doorway in my home,
But this one is different and leads to a place that
I call hope. I toss my old doorway to the sea.
If it returns I shall greet it like an old lover
Who no longer has a place in my heart,
And with a gentle touch,

Tell it to leave.

Home

My home
Is distorted by design.
Its yellow wallpaper stares at me in the dark
Begging me to lose my mind.
I've prayed over its yearning and covered my ears
As the internal fights grew so loud my home
May have been a megaphone.
Something so small goes in and is magnified
Burning ants on its way out.
They grow to loathe the sun.
I am the sun
And I am the ant
And I am the child watching
Women hate their own skin
Learning to hate her own skin.
Hearing every little thing
Staring at mirrors realizing my house
Is made of straw and those kids have mighty lungs.
I was 13 when I skipped my first meal
And I've regretted it ever since,
My house is too big.
Its hallways echo reminding me of how empty I've been.
But downsizing only shoves me into ill-fitting boxes
With no room.
Perhaps I could make myself small enough to fit.
To draw and quarter each new foundational brick.
Until I don't recognize my home anymore.
It's so much easier to be lonely when all the rooms
Are abandoned and echo with the
Reminders of you, of me.
Or so I thought, but even as I
Huddle in hoarded corners
I cannot find peace in this.

I am a tourist in my own city, my own home.
I struggle to decorate because nothing
Can cover those cracks in the walls.
And? When it crumbles?

Demolished by doctors' hands
Telling my home won't hold out like this
With so little keeping it afloat.

I think I was afraid of confidence because
What if its alien hands were misplaced?
Maybe there is no such thing.
Either way.
I am rebuilding my home.
I place each full-sized brick with care
And ask for help with construction
As I go along,
My house is filled with working songs.
We sing as we paint my bedroom walls
My favourite shade of green
I was always too afraid to wear...
My body still doesn't feel like home somedays
And there are times I wish to shrink myself to
Reach a goal that doesn't exist.
But today,
I bought some flowers.
I placed them in the doorway as a gift.
To myself.
My body.
My home.

We are allowed to laugh

I wake up each day and wonder who I will be.
The depressed or the manic, the sane or psychotic.
They have been part of me for so long that I don't know if that's just me.
But I find humor in the pain as time goes on.
I laugh about the time I thought I could fly because the voices told me so.
Or when I have to check the door three times before I even go.
How I would call everyone beautiful but myself,
I find humor in every trauma on my shelf.
I seem o be collecting mental illnesses like pokemon;
Bipolar, Bulimia, OCD...
I wonder how to separate them from me
And my autistic neurodivergency.
But still, I laugh.
Through the pain.
Through the darkness.
Like a pirate cackling with her crew through a storm.
It may be a coping mechanism but it also got me through.
We are allowed struggle yet laugh.
Despair but smile.
Sometimes that's the first step

In
breaking
through.
I think for
the first
time,
I might be
breaking
through.

Jill Fernie-Clarke

Jill Fernie-Clarke was educated in Newcastle, Manchester and Leeds and in 2003 completed a PhD titled 'Francis Wheatley's *Cries of London* series, its history and meanings'. Jill's research interests are focused on representations of 'low life' her work has scrutinised images of the poor in eighteenth century popular prints; representations of the 'low' in Blackpool, and she has also published work on collaborative practice.

More recently she has been Head of Blackpool School of Arts; a member of the Executive at the Council for Higher Education in Art and Design(CHEAD) ; Vice-Principal at Cleveland College of Art and Design and prior to this she was Head of Research at Leeds College of Art.

Self-compassion

Taught to think of others
Put them first. Smother
Yourself and be last.
That's the past.
Are we not on a par them and I?
Why?
What for?
No more.
Doormat, dishcloth, mug.
Trampled, wrung out and drunk from.
It's wrong.
Breaking away from old patterns is hard,
And it's marred,
By years of conditioning, brainwashing, partitioning.
Addressing it is difficult, but its not impossible to see
That maybe life could be better for all,
If we could climb the wall.
Reach the summit and see the horizon
With a new vision,
In which we're all equal,
People.
No longer subservient, compliant reliant
On the approval that comes from being last,
And cast.
As the martyr, the doormat, the mug.
Hug!
Embrace self-compassion. It's a fashion.

Iveta Kraule

Iveta Kraule is a Latvian-born writer who currently lives in Preston, Lancashire. She is also a member of the Just Write workshop. Ivana loves her family, independence, flowers, poetry, French perfume, classical music, dancing and travelling in the sun.

Last but not least, good conversation, which Just Write provides for her!

Small Masterpiece

Happiness has a name, has hands and legs.

Happiness likes to chat, to run and jump, to splash water when having a bath.

Happiness sometimes climbs trees and breaks windows, when playing football with mates.

Happiness can be very upset about encouragement to go to bed, when the game just started.

Happiness can ask: "Mum, please, read again the fairy tale about Snow White and the Seven Dwarfs."

For every Mum and Dad, happiness is the most valuable and beloved in all the world.

Happiness is never enough, and never too much!

The sky is broken and I want to cry
No more remains to buy
From our love and happiness I will live
No more sadness to buy or give

When no souvenirs, no hope
But endless love weaves rope
To tie you up in my cage of passion
Who cares if out of date, this fashion.

We will meet, before the end of time
In a presence of happiness
Under broken sky
Our souls will cry

Let's feel tenderness
Steaming as a morning river
Heart hurts happily
Wind is unfastened. Why?
Pain goes by.

Dedicated to Ukraine

Last bullet stuck in barrel, silence
Brunch has a deal with lonely dove
No bombs, no fire, no more violence
Again, it's time for peace and love

Thank God

Thank God, I don't love you anymore
No sights, no lights, more catches me
Nothing to look forward for
Thank God, I don't love you anymore

To be in love means endless lying
To cry for flight, but end up dying
With you, soul is empty score
Thank God, I don't love you anymore

Jonny Cosmo

Jonny Cosmo is a poet, writer and a proud northerner from the city of Preston. Jonny has published numerous works, including three poetry collections: 'Genesis: In the Beginning of October', a book of daily poems which were written over the space of twenty-one days, 'Look Mum, I wrote a Poetry Book', a personal collection of poetry with illustrations from the talented Edie McCartney, and 'Death, Health and Solitude' a collection of poems written whilst experiencing lockdown. Cosmo has also published a collaborative novel, 'Catherine's Canvas', under the pen name T.M. Cooks. Currently he is working on his next anthology, 'Sick, Sad, and Screaming' and a children's novel.

His writings are inspired by the lived experience of neurodivergence, with the hope that in reading his work others may feel understood. Seen. Heard.

To quote Jonny himself, "with a pen, nobody is alone".
@JustJonnyThings

Inert superhero

This one goes out to every outcast and weirdo.
The ones who were ridiculed for their inner superhero.

You were always different that came as no surprise.
Maybe you hid away whilst the other kids played outside.

Now you're older, much more grown-er but still not a moaner,
because distinction chose 'ya.
And those kids who called you a loner, well they grew colder,
unmoulded soldiers, for the fight, that's always been a lie.

Now you're winning, 'cuz fittin' in has never been your thing, and
fittin' in is a thing, of the past.
Stand out not outcast, because you're distinctive by instinct and
disciples of the status quo are lost.

You know what lost is.
You know if you never were you couldn't have found your way.
You know you're not a lost cause, 'cuz the lost are the ones who
told you, you were.

Dreamers, dreaming dreams

We the dreamers
Who share a dreamed dream of interdependent dreams
Resolute on the meaning of symbols
Until another states what they mean

We the feelers
Who share a feeling felt
Fickle thoughts built from perceiving
Until the doors of perceptions melt

We the thinkers
Who share a thunk thought
At least we think so anyway
Ideals means shared thoughts

We the believers
Who share a belief that we know
That all thoughts, feelings and dreams
Are within our minds control

Hosts in a hell

The walls are torment and alienated isolation
But this is where we call home
Clawing at the walls just for stimulation
Apparitions of fingers to the bone

Ghost is what they call me
But I'm just the whisper of a witness
Whimpering against catastrophe
Catastrophe of a sickness

We speak so we may be heard
Seen or understood
But all that is ever received
Isn't what is felt in the blood

Sometimes we cast spells
Expressions through the pen
But all is lost in echoes of the empty ink well
The living truth dies at ballpoints' end

We hosts in a hell
We shackled by our own constructs
We serve only to be observers
We bare witness to our downfall

Together never to be
Ambiguous disassociation
Hell is what can be seen
Through the eyes of the beholden

Ode to irony

Just one thought
Each word becoming another
To again branch into another and another
A thousand branches, a single tree
A flood of thoughts rolling into the sea
One
Is two
Is three
I lost count
A single thought
A drop in the ocean
My mind is the sea
I am the sailor
In a boat of emotions
My heart an anchor
My focus the sail
But I can't pull up the anchor
It's too heavy to hold
Sitting in a motionless boat
Of emotions
Getting old
To chase the wind
I only need
Let go
I forgot what I was going to say

A.D.H.D. Society

Can we talk about this A.D.H.D. invoking society?
Let alone neurodivergents' diagnosed with abnormalities.
The system is built around always having more
If enough isn't enough you'll always feel poor
We are brains as well as people,
Minds as well as masks.
So, when one speaks of freedom,
Take note of that in the task.
Modern technology,
Mainly our phones
Is designed to steal autonomy
Keeping us in it alone
Adverts on the TV
Adverts on the web
Adverts consistently
Slogans in our head
Distraction for your attention
Is the ironic oxymoron of marketing
No wonder our retention
Declines as our time is harvested
Kids who can't focus
Sedated with speed
Cause less of a ruckus
When we give them amphetamines
So, the next time
You criticise A.D.H.D.
BLAME THE MARKETTING MIND
In this attention deficit society

00:11, A.D.H.D.

A. D. H. D.

Just four letters but they change how you think of me
Once bright, eccentric, charismatic
Now you question my sanity

Now you look at me as if to see a spanner in the works

As if me an individual, different than you, from birth, in life, in experience, in thought - as is everyone, even most likely differently taught

But four letters change all of that in a second and the exact thing that beforehand made you curious to know me now makes you uncomfortable because you wonder how they control me

What pills for my ills do I need to be subdued

How about just a hammer and chisel up my nose, clink, and you can bare me, am I scary?

See it's odd to think that the exact tick that distracts my attention is the exact thing that also heightens my perception... I over think...

See, because when I told you just four letters, your left eye twitched, you retracted your gullet, your brow raised-fell? I couldn't tell because in that millisecond you caught it and then you fought the urge to tilt up your head and look down your nose at me but you did, I saw it, by the minimal degree your face showed a decree of what you now think of me. But I'm used to it, it's hard

61

to understand what's going on upstairs in someone else's psych land, but every hand is still flesh and bone.

A. D. H. D.

Sometimes it makes work hard, doing work, finding work, keeping work, finding work again, again, again, again, again and again. I need a sick day please, a chill day, a free from stress day, because it's not easy to be me and for you I must be this thing that beeps, submits, smiles.

DECLARE YOUR MENTAL HEALTH

Why? So, you can discriminate under the table against my will because you think I'm less able, unless PR said you need a token in the workplace.

A. D. H. D.

That's what they call it anyway, this one thing, my first diagnosis but I could tell you I'm also depressed and anxious, apparently due to stress from having A.D.H.D. but how does that mean my problems are any smaller. How 'bout we add dyspraxia in there, hey I'm epileptic too but just by adding to this list you now can't resist to again and again change your view of me with each letter, you might think that I'm better off dosed, or locked up. You might feel empathy or are you sure it's not sympathy, please do not pity me can't you see for all its worth we are stood in the same room. None of this makes me better. If it makes you then by all means follow through with your reactionary thought but a book is far better than its blurb.
Astounding, you couldn't wait to read the next page, truly one of a kind. 1/5 went off on tangents a lot couldn't follow.

A. D. H. D.

We're all different. Even as newborn infants.

Can't we just wait a little longer, read more than the cover, give at least the first page a chance, before we put the book back down, judged at a glance.

A. D. H. *Me.*
A. D. H. *We.*

In a world where nobody can look up from their phone screens, constantly flicking through images, messages, articles and games. To resort back to our dwellings, or sitting with family or friends, to again stare back at our screens, with another screen for background stimulation, because silence has become so unbearable.

Only a maniac would tell a child, deficit of attention with energy and determination to match a jet engine has a disorder.

Harriet Skully

Harriet Skully is an artist and writer who currently resides in Preston. She writes openly about her diagnosis of Schizophrenia and autism. Harriet's writing revolves around experiences of mental health illness and times spent inside psychiatric hospitals.

In her work, she likes to think about existences on the fringes of society, and the subtle threshold between creativity and 'madness'.

Medication

Clozapine coursing through my veins
Making me drowsy
Making me sane
So many pills
The count I have lost
Alas, sanity comes
At such a high cost

Melatonin for my circadian rhythms
But my mind is still wrought
By a thousand schisms
It helps me to sleep at night
But I wake up violently
At dawns first sight

Bisoprolol for my racing heart
Whilst my racing mind
Still falls apart
Racing thoughts in a racing world
Watch as death and life
Furl and unfurl

Aripiprazol, another anti-psychotic
Is my mind really
That chaotic?
Now I am restless as a hungry ghost
I seem to need the least
Yet want the most

Sertraline they say will lift you up
But alas I still stare
Into that half empty cup
And though I seem to be having fun
Deep inside

I am still numb

And even though they help, these pills
I look at the walls
Centipedes crawling still
Into my eyes and into my brain
Alas I admit
I must still be insane

I've lost myself, I've lost my name
Traversing the madness planes.

The madness mountains, the madness sea
Madness is the world to me.

So, come with me whilst strength remains
To traverse the madness planes.

Though some of us are happy here
The madness planes are steeped in fear.

Bring out your children, bring out your dead
The madness seas are crimson red.

Red with rage, red with blood
The madness streets begin to flood.

The madness streets that I have walked
As madness people start to talk.

Madness thoughts and madness words
I live where madness can be heard.

The man on T.V. says again
That we are in for madness rain.

As I walk, I get wet through
And know not where I'm going to.

I feel that I am lost once more
Washed up on the madness shores.

My feet are sore, my clothes are soaked
The madness shores sure are no joke.

So take my mind and take my hands
As we travel through the madness lands.

None of us

None of us here are people,
We are patients we are problems,
None of us here are people
We are complicated products

None of us here have agency,
To decide or to consent
None of us here have agency,
To refuse or to decent

None of us here have choices,
What to eat or what to wear
None of us here have choices,
What to think or what to care

None of us here are worthy,
Of regard or of respect
None of us here are worthy
We get dismissal and neglect

None of us here are crazy
We're not mad, we're not insane
None of us here are crazy,
We're just on another plane

A healing project

I weep from this skin, tender and raw.
Red tears from a body in pain.

My body is a healing project.
It takes the scenic route.
An entropic interplay of assembly and fragmentation

Blood clots and surface repair.

Scars are scrawled across my skin like stories on parchment.
Not stories of suffering, but of healing.
The ever-restorative nature of body, of flesh.
These lines depict a map, of madness I have travelled.

There was a rupture of thought, a tearing at the thin membranes
of mind.
Which not reassemble endlessly from the tattered rags of a
psychic flesh.

To heal, is not to return to the old skin, but to embrace the new
skin.
To traverse its surface.
Not a clean plane, but one on creases, of folds, folding and
unfolding,
of harrowing heights and unfathomable lows.

Maya Ozolina

Maya has always been a storyteller. From age five until the age of thirty-five, Maya danced and later taught others. She also choreographed dances for a living, but stories were always there. At four years old, when her auntie's boss ignored her, she threw flowers under a train. She was serious, even then.

Maya came to live in England in 2001. She came to improve her English and attend creative workshops as part of a festival, which happened to be next door to her. So she joined in. Her first written story was published in the groups booklet. She was hooked. Maya then moved to Preston and joined a group named 'Reading the World'. It was a group that focussed more on writing *and* performance. She later joined the Just Write group and has been a member for ten years now. The group published two flash fiction anthologies, 'Christmas shorts' and 'Love, literally', which she contributed to. Then, five years ago, she took over the Just Write group.

Maya has also written three short plays, two scripts for short films and created scenarios for three music videos. All which were produced.

She now focusses mostly on poetry, writing and taking part in open mics and other events.

Crying

Today I apologised for crying,
To the person who is closest to me.
I know, I should not apologise,
They would understand.
But I could not help it, both
Crying and apologising.
Maybe I should've done it earlier.
Much earlier.
The crying bit.
When there was less
Accumulated in my heart.
Before all the pain and sadness
Hadn't grown so big,
That I am not able
To simply cry it out
In one go.
It should be simple,
It must be simple
To cry it all out.
It's not.
Sorry!
and they said:
You just cry it out
On my shoulder,
Ok?

Fight

Fight!
Fight what?
The doom and gloom.
How?
Smile, laugh, hug, kiss, love!
What if I don't have a lover?
Get a cat or two!
Will the cat love me?
If you love the cat, it will.
I don't know, would it work?
Give it a try, get out of the darkness!
Ok?

Dream

Dream my girl, dream big!
What about?
All the best about!
What is it?
It's in you, dig it out.
How, with what?
With intention, with belief, with trust, with love!
Come on, you don't need a shovel for that!
Just your heart.
You are awesome, you can do it!
I am not even exaggerating, and never lying.
You know that.
Mum, whom are you talking to?
To an old, wise woman.
Talking to yourself again?
Yes, and what? Give it a try, it works!
Dreaming, discussing the plan, going for it.
It works.

Always!

Telling to myself

Stick to who you are, my darling.
Stick to who you want to be.
Go explore and learn, and grow.
You can do it, you old soul.
If you doubt it, it's alright.
Ask some questions to yourself.
Seek for answers, they will come.
You are stardust, you are awesome!
Your soul knows all the answers.
You just listen, you just trust!

Thanks!
I hope you enjoyed it?!!
Maya

Steve Rowland

Steve Rowland lives in Blackpool. He is a member of the Lancashire Dead Good Poets and Preston-based Damson Poets, which holds monthly open mic events on the last Wednesday of the month. He is a columnista for the Dead Good Blog for which he writes every Saturday; this can be found online.

He doesn't currently have a cat, it ran off with a seagull. He has never had a dog. He has at least two children and two bass guitars. His favourite colour is tangerine, and his star sign is Perseus.

Black Dog

When it followed me at first
I thought it must be
someone else's hound
lolloping soundlessly at heel
through the park at dusk,
but there was no one else around.

I shook it off that time
but when it joined me next
as I took my customary evening stroll
I guessed it must have searched me out.

Several times it even followed me home
and I figured it for a stray.
I always turned it away.

More recently I've woken
to find it waiting at the gate.
It never barks, just glowers darkly.
I'd put off venturing forth
till it was gone
although it sometimes made me late.

And now, I don't know how,
it's found a way into the house.
I hear it pacing, breathing,
right outside my bedroom door.

I think I'll never leave my bedroom
anymore.

Underdog

this is underdog
still trying to convert
the hounds he hears in his head
into poetry and song
soundbites howled with feeling
into unrequiting night
words punched out
through gritted teeth
in baskerville twelve point type

with the benefit
of hind-leg sight
he might not have cocked up
in quite the way he did
pissing opportunities
up the wall
in pursuit of
so singular a vision

but underdog
is not looking for your pity
as shorn of respectability
shunned by the pack
and shunning them back
he straddles a line
between genius and madness
underdoggedly
shambling towards epiphanies to be borne

Electropolis

The where, with all beyond recall.
The why, no matter anymore.
The who, well, there's the rub.
We came from out the sea,
We slept in caves, we lived in trees.
We must have loved, perhaps we cried,
Suppose we tried to live good lives.
Please don't attempt to read our thoughts.
You're breaking down an open door...
There's nothing left to free.
Identity parades elusively.
All else denied
But habit, steely instinct,
A segment of that circle which was lost
Rises hopeful still
From out the misty marshland
Of mis-remembered will
To span this chilling ether ridge
Into yon bold, bright Electropolis,
There to celebrate at last
The miracle of nostalgia with no past.

Debbie Razey

Debbie Razey

Debbie Razey, who writes under the pseudonym of Violet Moon Poetry, was born in Lancashire, England, in a village in the Ribble Valley.

Debbie is fascinated by nature and loves the great outdoors. She is also very interested in spirituality, and astrology, and is a huge music and poetry enthusiast. Debbie is an avid people lover and believes in peace, love and kindness - a bit of a wanna-be new-age hippie.

She once was a keen speech and drama student and has gained high-level LAMDA qualifications and starred in several dramatic productions. Debbie also worked for thirteen years with special-needs children as a communication therapist support worker; where she used her love of reading, drama, speech and music as a learning tool to communicate with and teach severely autistic children.

Debbie then turned her hand to writing poetry, which she now feels was always the direction she was meant to take as poetry has become a blessing and her lifeblood. You can find Debbie on her blog Aesthetica Poetica and also on Instagram (@violetmoonpoetry).

Still Life

Souls aching in emptiness
Drowning in vast voids of endless pain
Our fear, further fuelling... utter desolate hate

Lit pyres ignite more anger
Grief laden souls untethered, become
In vortex bereft of gravity, we... succumb!

Displaced dance in the darkling
Fell from the illumined, illustrious path
Ground beneath subsided... under heinous wrath

The dawn's lost notes are chiming
Calls us back to her bosom's embrace
Reminds us all of compassion; pure love... we still may taste

When warm tears cleanse from heaven
We no longer feel alone
Active our minds at slumber
As we thaw from bitter stones

Molten, upon horizon
Trapped hearts pirouette in clouds
Touch stars within each other
Caress away furrowed brows

Free to paint a new future
Bathe in sun's elixir kiss
Remove the past's spoiled tarnish
Let hope... fill up what's been missed

Won't you walk with me brothers?
Sisters, will you take my hand?
Let's follow in brave footsteps
Bleed forgiveness like the sand

Find truth in peace, serenity
In the lapping of the waves
Be whole in nature's wonders
Lift life out of trauma's stains

Clear our lens of perceptions
Find ourselves in solitude
With love's pallet, colour life
Paint in light, our dreary hues

Look upon your own reflection
Although distorted, is there light?
Because if there's still a glimmer
All's not lost... there is still life!

© Debbie Razey, 2020 (Violet Moon Poetry)

Crown of Thorns

A ring she dreamt; a crown of thorns she got
She loves so hard, yet still he spares her not
Her once full heart, he's tried his best to drain
Her mind hurts too; gaslighting fuels her pain
Romance she sought, not martyrdom for love
Punchbag she feels; cruel word-fists hit, ungloved
Trauma spits; injects... insidious doubt
From toxic seeds, her flashback roses sprout
Her fragile frame, reflects her gentle mind
She's desolate but all she has he finds
Red swollen eyes, sunsets bleed pleas for peace
Demons he heeds... she tries to make them cease
   Now crucified, she wonders why he leaves
   No prayers for her... will he spend down on knees

© Debbie Razey 2022 - Violet Moon Poetry

Jamie Field

Winner of the Disabled Poets Prize 2023 with his poem 'How to Sign a Playground', Jamie Field has had poems published in Banshee, Abridged, Magma and elsewhere. He is also a Poetry Ireland Introductions recipient 2021. Jamie holds an M.A. in Poetry from Queen's University, Belfast. He is originally from Pontefract, West Yorkshire. He currently resides in Blackpool, Lancashire.

Jamie began writing poetry at 27, his first poem being written by accident. From that day on, he was addicted to verse. As a deaf, autistic person, poetry is the closest way he has found to expressing himself authentically.

Jamie's all-time favourite poets include John Berryman and Al Purty. The writer he most enjoys reading is master of the long line, C.K. Williams for his authenticity that interests him greatly.

Changing Lanes

The moles on my arms are islands of an archipelago
the tip of my finger a speed boat running between,
in a box room I name them:
Butterscotch, St Luke's, New New England
and proclaim them mine,
brown mounds in an eggshell sea white,
give them history, economy, trade
broker deals with the islet on my right.
Adolescence, a storm arrives and cuts fault lines
the islands erupt red and a trench as deep
as the Mariana opens
the sea throbs and the sky moans
in the lull of a sterile ward heal,
porcelain seams in a scarred Sargasso Sea,
tanker in a groove journeying straight
days to brake, a life-time to turn around.
Age and independence a typhoon unrelenting
three parallel wounds dug to the core
primordial ooze bubbling, piano wire snapping
an ambulance at the door
islands drowning casualty of war,
in a world without corners
I guide my thumb over sea and terrain
feel for the certainty of shipping lanes.

Trigger Cuts

beneath a tiled victorian sky a lullaby
a murmur of sleepless nights and absent partners
interspersed with songs of wheels on buses
and an old man's farm
the littlest reaction a reason for the mothers to cheer
and when inevitably an almighty wail
blows through the grade II listed arches
the librarians sing: *awwww*
— every cry deserves a response
this I hear but cannot see
blinded by bookshelves: self-help and celebrity chefs
south wall where bachelors read the papers
and the motherless sleep
I can only extrapolate —
a woman gathers her child draws them in
snug below the shoulder blade — discharged
in time — on their way
to becoming someone
the mind flows —
try to dredge the specifics of memory:
the season — the light in the hallway
the depths a shadow makes as it tip toes from room
to living room — from brownfield to pennines
properties of a tear coalescing on a pillow
sharpness of silence made real
by the peaks and troughs of a hundred white lines
I read like braille —

Jade Kosa

Jade Kosa is mysterious. Her poetry and creative writing is deeply inspired by rock music. She tends to lounge about with the rain-dogs, and anyone who has ever been labelled weird by people who deem themselves ''normal'', (it takes one to know one).

What should I change about me?
Everything.
Every little square inch, down to its millimetre.

Through to my bones.
Into the essence of my
D.N.A.

Fingerprints.
Footprints.
Dental records.

Striving in a world of perfection.
I see my lack.
So, take an X-ray
and blot that out too.

But that's enough about me,
what about you?
Would you change every detail about you, too?

Hey! Wait!
Let's stand this on its head.
Couldn't we do something kinder instead?
And surely can't we see
about you and me
that it is by our imperfections,
that we are made perfect
and free.

Take the time
Take 10%
It wasn't meant to be taxed
By a matter of fact
And if you squander
All his portions
Relating to your failures, and
Without caution
Save yourself in your hour of life.
Pick up the pen
Put down the knife
And smile secretly to the clock of time
Melt sublimely
Make your world to rhyme
And when the great spirit
Calls you home
Write a book
To call your own
And your story will be added
To your history of birth
That justify your time spent
On this Earth
Sign your name
Upon the edges
Taking stock of all your vows
And pledges
And without hate
To not despise
Look your creator straight in
Her eyes
As judgement flickers through
The ages
Write your truth in worldly pages.

"You saved my life!"
I said, looking into their eyes
Scraped me up from the gutter
Face first in the dirt
Mouth full of gravel
Lifted from the ground
Laid me upon the silk scents of flowers
And let me sip sweet nectar

"You saved my life!"
I said, looking into their eyes
Loved me when I felt unlovable
Held my weak and fragile frame
Gave me sanity when I felt insane
Empathised with my cruelty
Forgave me when I fucked up
Rocked me to sleep
When I was afraid

"You saved my life!"
I said, looking into their eyes
Understood my afflictions, my
Compulsory lies
My addictions, my uncontrollable sighs

"You saved my life!"
I said, looking into *my* eyes
An angel within
And a whisper from the wise.

Angela Sherrington

I'm Angela from Preston Lancashire.

I've been writing poetry since I was very young,

I remember writing in class and for my family,

my silly comedic rhymes about the teachers, and life in general would always bring a laugh this gave me encouragement and confidence in my younger years.

The power of words can bring a tear or a smile,

they can stir emotions and help us know ourselves.

To scribble thoughts onto paper can be a very cathartic release.

I would encourage everyone to write.

Just grab a pen and start to scribble.

It helps.

Disassociation Poem

Bus journeys

Wheels in motion

I'm led in your bed trying to remember when we last spoken

Years of horrors our traumas manifest

Under the guise of we just need a rest

The window frame seams come unstuck at the ends

Oh hello darkness my old friend

No fumbling just stumbling on words which don't trigger

But hey look my boobs do look bigger

Small talk gets deeper the slope gets steeper god pass me a sleeper

this fear of each other. Damn—

James blunt - goodbye my lover

resounds in my mind yet Alone I'm crucified

hands tied should of never lied now my brains fried

And I'm back near home

 memories I keep

my time travelling mind feels like

so quantum leap

Auto pilot in charge of this plane

 disassociation can drive one insane

 but to me it my super power yet it makes me nauseous

But fuck your diagnosis

experia Aladocios

Nearing my home how did I even get here this magic ability gives
me no fear

For I know my splitting could cause spitting in one who can fit in

So yea the mental health team still holds down the tables,
diagnosing us all as mentally unstable

but people are people and it's clothes that need labels

So if your diagnosed mental ill

Have your not just like neo took the red pill

My ego will always make light of this fact and sadly it's then that
my sanitys hacked

Scary thing I know I am crazy

But damn at least my brain ain't lazy

Breakdown

Sitting facing yellow street

coffee bitter taste so sweet

Another year another tear

My heart and soul have full abandon

Yet doctors give me Prostaglandins

No thoughts anymore

The pain has sealed the door

 I'm praying one day a light will shine

The gap of my empty soul will rise

was my faith a sticking plaster to bring false hope to each disaster

was any of it real

Feeling dead yet being alive with sorrow

until you have died to No tomorrow

it ain't nothing to celebrate

Or make physicians contemplate the wonder of how I am still
here

It's not taught in psychology

How being alive after a lobotomy

 is worth the science of skilled hands

 yet I still stand

There must be a remedy from this internal madness

decomposed in sadness

I suppose

There' must be a hidden note a jigsaw piece an antidote to spark a
beat

not just d minor

So if the cure requires a deal

I'd hack off my limbs for once to feel

Again like before

But as I wander aimlessly for my search for some mortality

This thread of hope is all that stands

The veil is torn it sets a precedent

With human flesh I'm decedent

Do the deceased really need to fear

And that's my prayer to those who will hear

That you see my eyes don't glisten

That you realise I can't envision

For I know why people sell their soul

With none to give I've paid the reaper

I'm hoping on a pill that's sweeter

And if you know the remedy

In true fb style

dm me

Joel Tangham

Someone still learning how to communicate and
find the right words.

Song

I looked in your eyes

and our fingers touched

and I thought

I am no longer alone.

we are two and full of joy.

I stood in the raw fresh air and breathed

the first new breath in a long time

and was happy

inside

and out.

And we grew out and stepped out of shadows

with hope

and madness and joy

into the brightest sunshine

but as life's veins pulsed,

you wanted to share a beautiful sacred deep honesty.

And I wanted it too.

To transcend everything

to be so close that we were inside out

We shared that moment when you emerged

and spoke together, so warm, trusting and close.

Then I spasmed

heart gaping, bleeding in every colour

unable to breath.

My secret rawness

revealed.

Perhaps I should have sought help,

to find how to live with that wild neon rainbow of desolation

that ripped me open

unable to handle

how freedom in closeness

delved deep into my rawness.

And in time you grew to fear my festering, easily cracked scabs.

And watched yourself.

Holding back, tense.

Steering a ship near shore, always looking for rocks, always held
responsible.

And you tried to make me happy.

But it wasn't good for you

and my shining butterfly

you faded and shuddered and cried.

And I dropped everything and came close

with all the love that was in me.

And wrapped around you.

It became a way of life,

to not keep anything that I could spare.

I became hollow, and brittle.

But I would have done it forever, in hope that we could be what
we always were, deep down:

The most wonderful beautiful energy

weightless and full of love.

But I was the poison.

I couldn't heal myself, and so you could not be free. With me.

So you sought light and your true self,

in open daylight escape. In the same room, but with others, far
away.

But it hurt so much, that I could only watch the shadows upon the wall.

Always wanting to join, to be invited.

Bitterly jealous at my exclusion.

My wound rotting, seeping, forming growths, was there to see, reflected in your eyes, and heard, echoing in conversation.

In the end, I thought that if I gave enough, bent enough,

stretched enough.

Dug deep within, and gave it without ceremony,

we could start again.

But it was too late. I stood in my sparest form, forged of love, and you smiled calmly, tired and thin, fresh from your trip to new places. With your new wings of new colours, carefully sewn for more new journeys. Without me.

My neon, pulsing, toxic, loving heart burst, sloshing upon the ground, oozing from my sightless eyes.

And I went home, to work out what to do

With my frozen pose of loving, strained shelter.

With my despairing, wretched, bewildered loss.

With seven years of memories.

With my secret rawness.

[This page has been left intentionally blank]

Printed in Great Britain
by Amazon

45747715R00059